Grigori Grabovoi

THE TEACHING OF GRIGORI GRABOVOI

ABOUT THE SOUL

Author's seminar held by Grigori P. Grabovoi

on August 5, 2003

Translation from Russian into English

by Olga Toloshnaya

Eternal Spheres of Knowledge Publishing (P482UK)

GRABOVOI ®

Eternal Spheres of Knowledge Publishing

https://www.facebook.com/GrabovoiEternalSpheresOfKnowledge/
https://eternalspheresofknowledge.com/

2018

G. Grabovoi

The Teaching of Grigori Grabovoi about the Soul. – 2018 – 28 p.

<u>Publisher's Note:</u>

"What if your life so far has been just a preface to reading this book?"

Here, Dr. Grigori GRABOVOI's position on the Soul formulates the technology of the work of the Soul, doing *a most wondrous job of transformation by providing actionable knowledge in ways that encourage control and instant action. Implementing this knowledge attentively, its complex simplicity as if ignites a very insightful process and experience, while also making absolute sense in terms of its axiomatic principles, their application and of course, the results.*

ISBN-13: 978-1-9993649-0-8 (paperback)

THE TEACHING OF GRIGORI GRABOVOI ABOUT THE SOUL
August 5, 2003

Hello!

The theme of today's seminar is the Teaching of Grigori Grabovoi "About the Soul". This structure of the Teaching is based on the fact that when, for example, we consider my Teachings "On Salvation and Harmonious Development", in this case, the control element is primarily the task of saving all through the technology and use of different elements of control, for example, the Soul, the Spirit, Consciousness, body and so on. Exactly in my structural level of the Teaching "About the Soul" I first of all consider the work with one's own Soul, that is, a person works with his Soul, while doing the same tasks as well, for instance: the task of saving all, and also the task of personal control.

And when you are doing the control through the structure of the Teaching "About the Soul", first of all you consider the principle of similarity based on the fact that the Soul of man is built according to the same laws as the Physical Body of the One God. When you consider this position as an axiom, you see that the Soul is already eternal because it is built according to the same laws.

Therefore, when we consider, so to speak, the legislative level in the control, it turns out that in the conditions of control we see, first of all, when we consider precisely the development of the Soul, that the legislative level is seen here as the level namely of the action. And in the conditions of the control, it is precisely when we consider exactly my Teaching "About the Soul", here, first of all, the level of control is considered as the simultaneous level of action. That is, there is, in general, essentially no difference between control and action, therefore you have to be careful in terms of transitional boundaries, since only one optical level operates here. And in the conditions of this state, precisely the laws of the construction of the Physical Body of the One God are transformed in the form of the laws of building Consciousness, the Spirit, the Soul, for example, including the physical body of man.

And therefore, considering the legislative level of the action from the Soul, we can, first of all, see quite easily the elements in our own practice. For example, a treatment, yes? .. from an incurable, if it is a disease, it is clear that the eternal Soul is not susceptible to diseases. Then it turns out that, for example, going, for example, in the extrapolation level, as if at the level of the correlation of tasks, we see that the Physical Body of the One God is also imperishable, It cannot be destroyed. And it turns out that the physical body of man, which is like a projection, yes? .. of the Physical Body of the One God on the Soul of man (here, one must be more careful with the formulations, because the formulations are the element of control in this case) can also be indestructible, therefore, man should find, in Consciousness, just the point of non-destruction in terms of this position.

If the disease is somewhat complex, suppose it is complex, or some situation there, yes? .. is quite complex in terms of the need for a simultaneous and complex solution, for example, by many persons, then it turns out that by analogy with how the Physical Body of the One God does, we can act the same way by the Soul. And when you are listening to this lecture from the point of view of control, then your access, for example, yes? .. the access of your Soul into any situation is practically as instant as you have your imagination of how God also has the access practically instantaneous, right? ... to any point in space-time. Therefore, the instantaneousness of the action here is

4

achieved due to the comprehension of the moment of action.

That is, if you want to get the truth or knowledge in a more adapted form, yes? .. in a simple form, but that does not mean that it is not complicated. There might be simplicity, but complex simplicity, - then it turns out that you act by analogies. And so, if to transfer by analogy, for example, the control to the level of how human Consciousness works, it turns out that Consciousness should work in such a way that every element of perception is the restoration of man, that is, this is his life, this is his practically infinite development. And it turns out, man should move from self-perception towards infinite development.

And according to my "Teaching about Love" a person first of all follows the level of development of Love, therefore it turns out that the next development is Love, including the Love for oneself. And when you consider Love for yourself, for many, this process, in general, is rather abstract often. That is, there are a lot of people who are engaged, for example, in the field of rescue, in the sphere of life activity development, let's say, of civilization, yes? .. in their personal activities, they often raise the question: Love for oneself is like a question expressed in action. For example, the following action: a person went to make some purchase in a store, but how, for example, would he express this action, if he buys, well, suppose, something third, yes? .. not for himself and not for another one? Well, he can buy, suppose, a very complicated integrated board. How to express Love through this board? That is, the more technological the world becomes, the more kind of split the information of the expression of Love for oneself becomes.

So, in the Soul, Love for oneself, the same as Love for God, and in general, as for all taken together, let's say so, yes? .. for the whole World at once, this Love is one and inseparable. The Soul is the source of this Love, and then any board, any, let's suppose, system of the future control, or any cyborg-system is a substructure of the known initial point of this state of the Soul. And when you come for example, to the next level, yes? .. in cognition, in control, it turns out that it is enough to find this point in the Soul, and you get almost an instant access to any space-time through Love. That is, the Soul is actually the conductor of Love, moreover the conductor of that level that you receive, first, the instantaneous level of access, just as God does; secondly, affecting physical matter.

That is, God, how can He affect the physical matter, yes? .. He can manifest somewhere in the form of eternal physical body, well, can pass by in the form of the physical body of man. Then it turns out that this very walking in the form of the physical body of man is the development of the Consciousness of man based on the same type principle. That is, if a person sees that the body of the physical level is indestructible, that is, the Physical Body of the One God, for example, goes somewhere and buys something in the store, it turns out that by analogy the person understands that this substance exists, and he understands this at the level of the Spirit. In this case, according to my "Teaching about the Soul", well the Spirit acts in the form of a substance that acts and creates simultaneously. That is, if the Physical Body of the One God somehow affects reality and acts, for example, through the Soul of man, yes? ... through His Own Soul, then the Soul of man acts through the Spirit in this case.

And when we get such an expression kind of a linear one, that the Soul affects the physical reality by the Spirit, we get a rather specific mechanism of control, a certain form of the realization namely of the physical body of man.

6

Because the action on physical reality has a reverse wave: if you offered some effect on a plant, and the plant somehow improved, or grew, or you healed a person, for example, yes? .. and somehow improved the events, then you get back almost the same or more. And this kind of mechanics, yes? .. as if distributive from the point of view of some weighting elements, well, functional ones, or, so to say, of volumes of information, it can be very clearly calculated even based on the structure of the development of the Soul. That is, the Soul is a concept that is rather accurately manifested in human Consciousness.

But what gives accuracy to human Consciousness? So, in this case, it is clear enough that it is the Soul that gives accuracy in human Consciousness. And if we consider the structure of the development of the Soul, we see that the concept, for example, of accuracy in this case is the concept that carries as if an external element, yes? .. there might be different Worlds, different elements of control. So, in order to have, in these Worlds, as if an accurate element in one's own essence, in one's own personality, we must mandatorily, first of all, imply that accuracy is that characteristic that is present in us. Otherwise, we can walk for a long time around the infinite level of information.

And how, for example, to determine the position in the control accurately? So, in my "Teaching about the Soul" it is possible to do this control quite accurately, just by finding the projection of the Soul on Consciousness. And when we begin to analyze here, just a simple logic enables us generally to do the analysis, in fact. After all, human consciousness is what defines behavioral systems, yes? .. the situation in the World and so on. From the point of view of the Physical Body of the One God, the entire reality is His Consciousness: explicit, implicit, physical, for example, or informative. It turns out that the Consciousness of man is manifested, for example, in the action of God in this case. When you see the action of God as an element of Consciousness, you see that your Consciousness can also be infinite, the same as the Soul of man.

That is, you come logically to the fact that, by analogy, the projection kind of component of the Soul is also the Soul anyway. And it turns out that you are allocating a spectrum of linear, that is, accurate, correct Consciousness in your Soul. And you see then the sources of the growth of Consciousness, how the Soul creates Consciousness in general, and the same way, by analogy, the Physical Body of the One God creates any reality. You see, according to what laws your Consciousness develops. And the Soul has absolutely all knowledge about the future development. Therefore, when you see how Consciousness grows, you know exactly where it grows, and what you will perceive.

And by the way, as a practice you can use such an element that, following the lines of the growth of Consciousness, you should see the future development of your Consciousness in general, how it develops. And from the point of view of God, He created man who can adapt in general to any reality; hence the possibilities to develop Consciousness are infinite, the same as the state in which the Soul is. And taking into account that for the Soul this state is based on the platform, which is the Spirit, the omnipresent Spirit, including the Spirit of God, then for Consciousness this is development. Therefore, the world is arranged so that there are as if stationary, basic sources of reality, yes? .. The Soul, for example, the Physical Body of the One God; and Consciousness or the Spirit of God are the elements that can develop. That is, the Spirit of God can be developed, the Spirit can be introduced. God's Spirit can be brought in.

And when you make a prayer, you see that God, He is both ubiquitous, and He unequivocally talks only with you, yes? .. This is the element of the transfer of accuracy and kind of all-embracing system, that is, such all-embracing knowledge that you have, and you see practically unambiguously that He solves all your issues, can solve and solves. But when you appeal to Him, to God, you see that He gives you knowledge, that is, development. And by analogy with this, we see the development of our own physical body. That is, I have come to the physical body of man through a rather multi-tiered kind of level of control that, at this given point, expresses the beginning of the construction of the body.

Therefore, the body is a very multi-component, as if an informative construction in terms of universal reality, and, from the point of view of the Physical Body of the One God, there is a difference here precisely in perception. The Physical Body of the One God exists and that is all. That is, it would seem, man as if should not build It, yes? And in principle, he may not build. But if he begins to build in the same way as the Physical Body of the One God functions, to build the World this way, yes? the World that surrounds him, then the World arranges the circumstances of development around him so that his body becomes eternal. Here in my "Teaching about the Soul" - and here I will say more precisely - about the Soul of man, in this part we are talking about the fact that the construction of the external World, that is, the construction of the events of the World, creates namely the line of development, that is, in fact, kind of the destiny of man.

And when you look at reality with your eyes open from the point of view - open from the Soul, then you see that all external objects of reality: such as animals, yes? .. suppose plants, some other immaterial and material objects - they have a source that is comparable and juxtaposed to the

Soul. You can tell that there is, suppose, yes? .. the Soul of animal and so on. But when you start looking closely at how generally the Soul, for example, of animals, reacts to some situation, you can understand clearly how it reacts exactly in the equilibrium processes of the World, if you see how the Consciousness of animal develops.

That is, this is the Consciousness of the animal that holds, as if, yes? .. the whole construction of the World in development, including the same way as any element of information that holds the entire external World in a single point precisely according to the structure of the "Teaching about the Soul". Then here you can, coming out along the boundaries of the development of the Consciousness of animal, but exactly from the development of the World - be more attentive here - for man the development of Consciousness proceeds from the Soul. When you want to understand how the outer element of the World sees, yes? .. and to control the element, naturally, as the Physical Body of the One God does, you must see how the World shapes the development of Consciousness of animal, or of a plant and so on. And when you see this difference, you understand what is the difference between God and man. And when you see so, you can follow the path, along which God walks himself and His Physical Body walks, then you can develop the structure of the Soul, that is, you can influence the structure of your Soul.

This is a principled, generally speaking, knowledge, because the influence on the structure of the Soul of your own or of another person is what God does unequivocally. There are things where only God Himself does the work. And when you, for example, do it the same way as God does, then you come into the structure and into that World, so to say, into the fundamental system of the Universe in general. And then you can influence any molecule, for example, any macro-system only because you perceive this system the way you want. The area of desire here, that is, the sensual desire coincides with the area of actions and the realization of actions.

Thus sometimes there is, well, say, such a sign in perception that when you want to perceive, for example, some process and want it very much, it can be realized. This is happening in the Soul of man. And when you, for example, want to set your action, for example, the action of the resurrection of a person as a goal of control, then in this case you can realize this for yourself, because man, according to the Soul, is the same as the Physical Body of the One God. And the Physical Body of the One God creates reality. Therefore, according to my "Teaching about the Soul" it is sufficient to develop the Soul to the level of realization of reality towards the norm, towards the Physical Body of the One God and people will be resurrected. That is, it turns out that, in this case, the action of control is only an act of striving for the Physical Body of the One God: either of physical striving, or striving by the Soul, that is, the principles are balanced here.

And that equation, say, equalization of these principles is the space of development of your Spirit. That is, I introduced such a concept as "the development of the Spirit" in the information or in the space of the Soul. And here we see that the two neighboring elements of your Soul, although they are a single whole and are inseparable, is that which contains the Spirit between them. When a person makes a prayer, and appeals directly to God, he first of all sees as a kind of an optical element, of the message, a spiritual characteristic, since the Soul is already with God.

The Soul is always near God based on the essence of creating the physical body, that is, there is that space where it always happens. And people are inseparable, for example, with the Creator, just as each of your cells is inseparable, in fact, with some other cell. When you come to the analogy of the construction, or the structure of the physical body, you see that, for example, the restoration of the body, or, suppose, of an organ, or, restoration, in general, of a person is an action that comes from every cell of your body, and moreover [it occurs] exactly according to the same laws based on which the Physical Body of the One God is developing, that is, the Physical Body of the One God, moreover is such one that looks, for example, like man.

Simply put, if we consider the situation of development from one cell, for example, to other information, how does a cell generally interact with another one? Then it is possible to consider here such a principle: a kind of light glow comes from the Physical Body of the One God, which by some laws falls on some object. And this object, as it is organized, yes? .. by the very God, so, it turns out, it is controlled by God as if in the future time. It turns out that the moment of creation and the moment of the following control is one action for God. And there is only Light between these actions, actually the Light of knowledge, the Light of knowledge of all people, of all kind of the elements of the World, about what is happening in general, or self-awareness.

And this element of self-awareness is actually the cellular level of man. That is, each cell in fact, based on the level, for example, of the action from God, is at the level of constant self-awareness, that is, it turns out it is the intellectual level of the cell, and generally, of the atom or the molecule of man. This is really a very high level in terms of intellect. If we consider this level as a level comparable to the action of the Physical Body of God, then the laws are clearly seen: how a particular cell interacts with a concrete element of reality, that is, with a neighboring cell, with an organ, for example, with a structure that is external in relation to the human body.

And when you start analyzing this way, you see that, generally speaking, any cell is restorable because it has a direct contact with God. And when you come to the level of this contact, you see that for God it is absolutely indestructible. And these data are in your Spirit. You begin to transform this Spirit and as if extrapolate, project it to Consciousness, and you get a dynamic system of Consciousness development in your Soul. That is, what I have said up to this point - this is a static structure, you see how the lines of Consciousness develop as if on a platform, yes? ... at the level of the Soul. And the dynamic system is like moving, let's say, blocks of light, of information, which have multi-syllable functions. It is not kind of a linear system yet.

And when you begin to develop your Consciousness further, or to consider the level of control from the point of view of adaptation, for example, how can you do so that there is no global catastrophe when you have the knowledge about the Soul? Here, it turns out, it is enough to take the static linear function, to develop it to the level of dynamics and to see precisely the manifestation of Love from the action of your Consciousness, because the manifestation of the action of God is Love. And when you, connect all this, as it seems, in such a simple logical scheme, you get that you can develop Consciousness to that level where you are truly indestructible, you can heal any other, yes? .. person, you can carry out a control of an event.

And if there is such a nuance, why, for example, do we say that the knowledge of this type, as if, yes? .. it would seem - just to develop and do - often does not bring quickly to the fact that a person heals instantly or prevents any catastrophe. Because God gave everyone the similar task in fact, yes? .. in the whole World, that is, the development of the World, and the same Soul in terms of tasks. The task is one, that is, man must be able to live eternally, and he must know this knowledge, how to do it. Therefore, if someone has not learned, you can prevent catastrophes, at least globally and accurately with the technologies, say, of direct control, yes? .. according to my Teachings. But in order to find the tasks of the personality, one must obtain access to the personality.

In my "Teaching about the Soul", it is so that in order to cure a person, it is necessary first of all, that his Soul wants it. That is, there is a principle of free will, and the Soul should want. If we consider the process ideologically, that the eternal Physical Body of the One God gives eternal development, it turns out that the Soul still should want it [to be cured] somewhere there, yes? .. in the future or in the past. That is, there is an element of desire. So, this element of desire is the birth of a person. A person even before physical birth never comes to Earth without the primary desire expressed by him personally. And, in this case, the expression of the personal desire and the expression of what God created, including the Soul of man, rest on the task of development of the World. That is, the personality makes the decision even, it turns out, before the element kind of creation seen by man. There are very subtle [structures], or subtler structures occur, because the Soul is a subtle structure, this is a multi-complex structure.

Before the element of creation there is the World of the Spirit of man, not of spirits of some kind, but of the Spirit of man, who must be born. And this World, this is what God perceives, the Physical Body of the One God perceives the spiritual aspect of man. The Spirit is, first of all, as an element of perception of the future. Because where there is no past, yes? .. the future, and the present, we get practically, in general, the level of control, which is typical of the everyday level of the cell. For example, if to think about the situation for a cell, say, of a person, yes? .., then the concept of the future, the past, and so on, of the present, is the same neutral concept as for God, who builds all reality. Because the cell is also as if located inside the system.

Also, the Spirit, which is in the infinite aspect of interaction, for example, with other elements of the development of reality: for example, people have already been created, yes? .. some number of people. So, the Spirit of these people interacts with the Spirit of that person who is not yet born, as if not even created. And it turns out - why is it often hidden from man, for example, yes? .. or perhaps why man does not generally reflect on how the Soul of man is created? Because it is the prerogative of God, He created, and that is it. And this parameter is distanced because a person does not think, maybe, often over simple truths, even because of the specifics of his activity, yes? .. for example, he is an atheist or he is very busy. Not because he cannot do this, he simply does not raise the question that the Spirit, in fact, which has an infinite kind of optical visualization that is generally informational, is in the future as well.

Therefore, a man who has not been created yet, yes? ... the Soul that has not been born by God has already a contact with the future World. And for God, this is the construction of His Physical Body. That is, the Physical Body of God is built up due to the fact that the elements kind of the information that are not yet created, already exist and intersect with future processes. And when you see such a level, you see that man always consciously chooses his own way from God, that is, well, eternal, yes? .. development, of eternal life. When you see this, you can convince in general any other person, that if he initially personally chose this way for himself, then he must live eternally, that is, it is kind of a simple logical scheme. Although to bring closer to this scheme, it is necessary as if to do many additional actions, sometimes it can be a simple algorithm, sometimes it is a complicated one.

If, for example, to state what I have said, well in written words, yes? .. because still I create the seminar at this moment, the topic of the lecture, the lecture itself right now, and if to write it down later, and to try to do it in the form of axioms, it will not be difficult in fact. There will be a number of rules, axioms, for example, yes? .. of principles, methods, and that's all. And using such a system of evidence, giving it, for example, to such a person who needs, for example, to be healed, yes? .. this system, - he will read it, and he will step on the path of life. And the Soul begins to heal the body, it turns out. So, the process of healing the body is the normalization of the World, just as God normalizes the World. For God, there should not be sick bodies, in fact, or those who can have problems with life.

So, the norm is the way how God does the norm, how the plant grows, yes? .. how animals grow, how generally the world is transformed, how generally a person breathes - this is the technology of self-recovery of man. And when you start to consider it this way, it is possible, for example, you consider such a process where, suppose, to consider the monetary phase of the development of a social society: why is money needed? If before the beginning of the development of all elements of information, prior to the beginning, yes? .. of the creation of man there was the question of the primary level of information where money was not needed. Why does the distribution system now require money, yes? .. and so on? And when you begin to analyze, you see that in order to save the World well, for example, with money, yes? .. that is, having accumulated, it is necessary to save money for rescuing the world, for example, yes? .. having set such a task, then the purest path, namely, aimed at salvation, is the path that comes from the Soul of man. That is, a person acting by the Soul, who is as if contributing to the financial system, for example, in the system of access of information, has more tools in such a case. Or if to put the Soul into equipment, it turns out, the equipment does not destroy.

That is, any systems of interaction, kind of monetary, informational, well, monetary in terms of control of some processes of information transfer, yes? .. Money as information, as a flow and transfer of information. Or for example, equipment like a system of informative access, that is, a plane has arrived somewhere, a person as if, yes? .. has overcome the distance. When we consider the questions precisely in such a way that, for example, we spiritualize through the action of the Soul, then we get that, the further we move, the more the World will be still diversified, that is, the more intersections of some kind will be there, yes? .. informative, technogenic ones, and so on. Therefore, the World will still develop in terms of maximum interaction. And the very maximum of the interaction is what God practically gives to man in the form of eternal development. That is, the number of events accumulates, so that a person still lives eternally. And when you know the technology of working from the Soul, every event leads to the fact that you comprehend this essence: that is, each following event leads to an even greater comprehension of the elements of eternal development.

And, proceeding from this, if we set the task in general so, and generally reason in such a way that is how then does a person, for example, view God, yes? ... from the point of view of Consciousness created by God? After all, it turns out that the function of Consciousness is anyway determined by God from the very beginning. The principle of freedom, in this case, gives free will to man as well, that is, a person while reflecting on how God created him first of all considers the element of analogy, for example, the Physical Body of the One God. It is simple enough, it is logically simple, for example, to assume that eternal God, who has the eternal Physical Body, naturally created the likeness, well, let it be the Soul. But in fact, this is really so, that the assumption, it turns out, yes? .. is the fulfilment, that is, the real event.

And why is it really so? Where is the criterion, yes? .. of this reality? In order to make some criterial, for example, conclusions at a kind of multi-plan level of control, it is necessary to practice. That is, for example, the fourth stage of cancer is cured when we think like this. And then we cure, for example, any person, yes? .. and then we, for example, do not get sick. And the criterion of this true reasoning is the fact that we, following the will of God about, for example, eternal development, do the normalization, yes? .. of the external World and of the internal one. And when we move on to the concept of the inner World, we see that the Soul actually illuminates the body from the inside all the time.

For example, there are more questions, probably in childhood, for example, I was interested somehow in the question, because, for some reason, I was asked in childhood, "Where is the Soul?" The children just came up to me and asked: "Where is the Soul?" And I, at that time, saw a specific, local location of the primary kind of, yes? .. level of glow in the body, for example, in mine. But at the same time, I somehow tried not to answer the question so clearly, but rather softly said that it was necessary as if to

18

think how to apply this knowledge in general. Somehow, I answered gently this way.

And if, for example, to ask the question now this way, yes? .. in principle, it is still the same, right? .. although, it would seem, it is about childhood, well about some age when children ask. The unequivocal answer will still be a kind of a very local one. Yes, of course, the Soul is manifested in man, that is, it is, naturally, yes? .. in man as well, and first of all in the only kind of level, that is, in the physical body of man. But, so to speak, that it was somewhere locally? It is possible to see it: the first access is according to the first manifestation, which is the glow in the heart area, yes? .. from the glow of your own Soul. When you get into the depth, well into the space, which is practically infinite, and it, this your system of perception, immediately begins to react, that it is really very deep, that is, your Soul, it is simply bottomless, it is very deep.

And when you start thinking like this, you can achieve the contact with God as well. God, He also gives the first manifestation and there is an outlet onto Him, right? ... as into the infinite system of knowledge. And here it turns out that there is a personal aspect of communication with God. And, in an infinite system of interaction, there is always a place for concrete action based on the mutual desire. That is, for example, you want to resurrect or cure there, and God, of course, wants it - it is clear from the beginning, once you are created. It turns out that there is only one way, that is, you need to find the way, which God gives, in fact, in all elements of reality.

And here it turns out that the knowledge about the creation of man, for example, about the creation of the Soul of man, yes? .. as the areas of space, this is the knowledge that people can perceive, for example, in such a way that, say, if you show this space, where the Soul is being created, well, to the perception of man, man may not approach it further as if by logical reasoning, because his logic is constructed exactly here. And it turns out to show the mechanism of creating the Soul, it is necessary to develop the logic so, that the logic, the Spirit and the Soul were one. And this is the physical body of man. It is only the physical body that collects together, yes? .. such different concepts, different systems, from the point of view of creation by God. And when you see this reality, it turns out that the physical body must participate, or co-participate in the process, well, let's say, of the World creation, in the process of the interaction of such levels as the Soul, the Spirit.

And here it turns out that you can act on your own, knowing the way how God acts, how the Physical Body of the One God acts in these circumstances. For this, you need to understand what the Physical Body of the One God considers as a given circumstance: to act from one's own Physical Body, where the body is the expression of unity. And that's why, according to my Teachings, I always show that the Eternity of the physical body is very powerful, often it is the only instrument of cognition that will really make it possible for the civilization to be saved. Because if we do not consider the element of the Eternity of the physical body as an element of eternal development, then we always come to the notion of finite quantities, with quite an indefinite system of development behind them, yes? .. And it turns out that the element of Eternity in this case is manifested as an element of universality, that is, the element of knowledge transferability as well, for example. That is, the knowledge, generally speaking, that is from God must necessarily be universal.

And that's why when, for example, we just walk somewhere along the streets, eat something or somehow react to reality, we get, all the time, knowledge that passes

20

through us and transforms, generally speaking, all the World, in fact. And when we want, for example, to understand, how this knowledge manifests itself in this concrete action, that is, where this knowledge is that enables you to influence the reality precisely near you, yes? .. Just take a closer look and you will see that it is near you, and you, in general, can understand it very easily, it is just enough to tune in to it and understand. The main thing is as if to see it nearby here, right? .. Nearby does not mean that only near the physical body. Nearby is where the Soul, Spirit, physical body, Consciousness and God work in one level.

So now I have cited in general the culminating important thoughts in this system of control in my "Teaching about the Soul" that at the level of the Soul, the Spirit, Consciousness, and the physical body of man, the Soul of man, God, the Physical Body of the One God can act simultaneously and synchronously.

And it turns out that any element of the World becomes exactly as you perceive it, that is, unambiguous, rigid, fixed in a particular place, and at the same time having complete freedom of will, yes? .. So, well, if this is some kind of object of the World, suppose a functional one, yes? .. for example, there, there is a recorder here, I can take it and move to another place. But it is kind of a technical structure that is determined to record sound, for example, yes? .. If we are talking about a person, a person has the full will to do what he wants, creatively in the first place, of course. And from God in general, he must act exclusively creatively.

When we consider an action: why are there non creative activities, such as wars, for example, yes? .. It turns out that the Soul of man, built in Image and Likeness, it turns out, of the Physical Body of the One God, it is exactly built. The physical body of the One God is precisely arranged as the physical body of man. And when we see these laws, we see that the interaction between the elements of the physical body of man, yes? .. and the outside World is often also traumatic: a person can hurt a foot, yes ... a finger and so on. But when we want that this does not happen, that is, in general, set an exceptionally unambiguous task so that a person does not get injured at all, does not get sick, does not get into accidental situations, and so on. In this case, it is somewhat idealized, but from the point of view of the exact future development, it is a task that must necessarily be solved, at least to begin with, for some situations, yes? .. so that there is no global destruction, so that the incurable diseases are cured, for example, and so on.

And when you come to this from the point of view, namely of the level of the Soul, it turns out that your Soul is the instrument that develops the World and it simultaneously develops in it from the point of view of the surroundings. After all, the Soul is given from God originally integral, having all the knowledge. Therefore, your Soul develops only with external observation.

And when you - for example, well, a person went to school, he learned something there, it is believed that he develops - and when you look at it well with your own eyes and see that development is only your perception, and not the perception of the Physical Body of the One God, it is clear that it is you who is doing this development. After all, a person sees from his Soul, what he personally does in this World, and consequently you bring this development to another person, for example, to the World. And therefore, according to my "Teaching about the Soul" by the action of the Soul, you necessarily give actually the knowledge of your own, yes? .. to another person, and at the same time you perceive it as, in general, his own knowledge, that is, you do, generally speaking, by analogy with the Physical

22

Body of God. That is, giving to another one, you give him his property as an independent system, yes? ..

For example, well, in my technology, for example, of curing it is set that it is necessary to give the apparatus of knowledge that would enable a person after being cured, extrapolate the knowledge to any other situations: such as not to fall ill, treat others. That is, here is the principle of transfer - why do I exactly set it like this? Because, for example, according to my "Teaching about the Soul", the World is arranged generally in such a way, that in any case I act so that knowledge is necessarily transferred at the moment of action.

This is how the Physical Body of the One God acts: an object of reality is created at the moment of action, and it develops. Therefore, there is no time in action, there is no time. God is always with us, because He is always in this time. And our task is as if to understand, to enter into a synchronous level of interaction with Him: this is why, when making a prayer, many events improve for the person. Because, first of all, the global systems are clear here, what God wants exactly in the global understanding, specifically from each person. It is clear that He wants eternal development, that there should not be, yes? .. destruction, wars, that there should be creation, harmony, but locally, namely locally for every person. And then it turns out that you see practically every person, just like, for example, the Physical Body of the One God perceives, but you see it by the Spirit. The spirit is all-seeing.

That is, I have already passed to the next, qualitatively new level, that the Spirit, coming from the development of the Soul, is already all-seeing. Just the question is how, in general, to catch the reverse signal and to transfer to Consciousness. You see there this person, he needs help, you help him, for example, yes? .. and you may not notice this. So, in order to transfer to Consciousness, you can generally do so that, for example, in a dream, if you see some kind of dream, yes? .. and if there is some kind of projection of different events, then, in a dream, it is possible to transfer to Consciousness only, for example, in the form of a projection the good part, that is, to you, for example. You think that this part is useful for you, yes? .. and you as if shield some of it and make the content of the dream useful for your future events. If there is no dream, then it is as if just thinking.

And exactly this possibility to process kind of information in terms of positive control, well, as if throwing away nothing and as if generally touching nothing: you just start following that way that is the way of God. That is, you are as if walking along His tracks of the Physical Body of God, where there are no problems, no, for example, catastrophes, yes? .. and so on. And the more accurately you step on these tracks, the less problems you have.

So, if the supporting structure of this road is Love, and it, Love, is kind of a systemic basis of these, say, yes? ... tracks. Then you see the act of the creation, how God created and creates you. And every element of this movement brings you closer to the act of self-creation. And if you as if the more accurately approach it, the more, for example, healthier you are, the more favorable events you have. It turns out, for you, the act of creation and act of action, the current action, yes? .. is the same thing.

Man is created by God as if simultaneously for all time and as if at the real moment, at the current time. That is, well, if we consider the situation in an abstract, in a complex way: He is some kind of molecules, galaxies and so on. After all, God is as if moving all this, yes? .. creates a trajectory for each element. Then every point of a person, every cell, is in an equivalent relation to the act of creation.

God creates man at every moment of time. And it turns out that if you consider this knowledge, how He does it, then through the structure of your own Soul you can calmly create your own body, create your own development. To do this, one only needs to know: how does God, that is, to what kind of core axis does He introduce the information, yes? .. How does He interact with you at all? The sources? And after all, God is completely open, He gives all the information to ensure that there is eternal development.

And when you begin to move, for example, along the way about which I have now told, then you see it as if the point of your Consciousness, or the area, yes? .. or, for example, the essence of your creation is you yourself: you, your action, your physical body. That is, you can perceive the body and immediately understand that you have done it, including the level of your own self-creation, this is your level, you introduced it to yourself. Going up, you see how God is doing it, yes? .. and God, He is just doing it more diversely, He is doing as if for all at once. Therefore, going even further, you start to do immediately, and for all, and for yourself. Then you come to the usual norm, which is not reflected in any way as an element of creation. That is, this is the normal state for you. Thus, the norm, this is when the element of self-creation happens as if without any problems, that is, when you do it, for example, correctly, yes? .. according to the knowledge of God.

And it turns out that to ensure that there are no deviations from the norm, you should consider the future trajectory of development, future events, and make these events such that you have your way as a path that you have already defined, which is already defined. So, the way, which is already determined, it is still in your Soul, God has already given you this way. So this is again approaching the Soul itself, yes? .. It turns out, like a sinusoidal rhythm, like the heart works: first you go to external control, and then again come to yourself. And this level is also the way of God. God develops harmoniously, the same way as, for example, the sinusoidal system of the work of heart.

And when you ... well, let's suppose, if we introduce a term sinusoidal, for example, harmonic, yes? ... let's say so, then we see that the process of control can be very precise in fact. That is, it is enough to introduce, suppose, the level precisely of this sinusoidal series, yes? .. into one's own Consciousness, that is, to project into one's own Consciousness, and then to be able to bring out, for example, this level, kind of the projection actual level, to the structure of the Soul. It is even possible to introduce a number series - that's why I often give a number series that makes it possible to reveal the healing level of the person, namely, of the Soul of the person.

There is a very strict system of measures like the Soul, it is an absolutely precise system of the World. And therefore, we get the control in such a way that we only enter the necessary tasks from Consciousness into the structure of the Soul, into the structure of the action of the Soul. And it turns out that we get, for example, our own healthy, yes? .. body, we can get, well, if we work long, then, for example, we can get closer to absolute health. If a person works less, he is more busy with other things, he can somehow, at least, heal himself, yes? ..

And when we come to such a concept: that if a cell is cured, or if a person is able to restore even one cell, for example, then there are no restrictions at all, he will completely recover. If he can restore himself by thinking, that is, practically by the element of the development of the Soul. Thinking as an element of the development of the Soul, considering here namely in terms of action, the development in terms of action and moreover of your personal action, and your personal development, it turns out that this can be transferred to another person. That is, all the principles of remote control, of saving, begin to take a very simple logic scheme.

And when you come to the fact that you get, for example, the control like, for example, a system of thinking, that is, thinking is an isolated system in this case, it is possible to make very static constructions in it, distribute to reality, and you will calmly get into any system of reality. You can see that when considering your Soul, yes? .. the Soul of the Physical Body of the One God, or considering, for example, any element of reality as a spiritualized element, you are quite able to get a completely accurate controlling structure, but which has more levels kind of the following development. Because it is not just a control as such, is it? .. This is the essence of the World, the truth of the World where the Soul is free, calm, developed in terms of the tasks of God.

And as an independent work, you should work out the following situation. Do so that the glow of the Soul, directed at the Spirit, Consciousness, the physical body, would be such that there is kind of the joint optics, yes, - you shine with your Soul onto the Spirit, Consciousness, your physical body - and the total optics would be directed exactly to the Physical Body of God, of the One God. And you will immediately see that you will get a very strong restorative, harmonious effect namely of eternal development.

This concludes my today's seminar. Thank you for attention.

ABOUT THE AUTHOR

Grigori P. GRABOVOI ® is an exceptional Clairvoyant Scientist, Doctor of Physical and Mathematical Sciences, Academician, with numerous Awards and Honours, Patent holder, Forecaster, Healer, Author, Artist, Advisor (Aviation federal services), .. as well as Individual Entrepreneur of "GRIGORII GRABOVOI PR Konsalting Technologies of Eternal Development" https://pr.grigori-grabovoi.world/
You can read his biography here:
http://grigori-grabovoi-education.info/biography-of-grigori-grabovoi/
As he states in his book "Unified System of Knowledge", GRABOVOI ©, 1996,p.8. : *"With my practical results, I proved the possibility of complete restoration of destroyed matter."* Here, it must be noted that Grigori Grabovoi provides systematically, officially documented evidence, in detail, as published in his books and websites. His technologies are empirical, confirmed scientifically, as well as spiritual in essence.

Grigori Grabovoi's system of knowledge is not just a general knowledge of his seminars material, but the material that is to be implemented in the form of concrete practical results. This means that the underlying aspect of his technology is PRACTICE, that is, obtaining the necessary results in a creative manner, finding significant application in daily life.